COUNTRY 🌐 PROFILES

COSTA RICA

BY ALICIA Z. KLEPEIS

BLASTOFF!
DISCOVERY

Blastoff! Discovery launches
a new mission: reading to learn.
Filled with facts and features, each
book offers you an exciting new
world to explore!

This edition first published in 2020 by Bellwether Media, Inc.

No part of this publication may be reproduced in whole or in part
without written permission of the publisher.
For information regarding permission, write to Bellwether Media, Inc.,
Attention: Permissions Department,
6012 Blue Circle Drive, Minnetonka, MN 55343.

Library of Congress Cataloging-in-Publication Data

Names: Klepeis, Alicia, 1971- author.
Title: Costa Rica / by Alicia Z. Klepeis.
Description: Minneapolis, MN : Bellwether Media, Inc., 2020. |
    Series: Blastoff! Discovery: Country Profiles | Includes bibliographical
    references and index. | Audience: Ages 7-13.
Identifiers: LCCN 2019001493 (print) | LCCN 2019002726 (ebook)
    | ISBN 9781618915887 (ebook) | ISBN 9781644870471
    (hardcover : alk. paper)
Subjects: LCSH: Costa Rica–Juvenile literature.
Classification: LCC F1543.2 (ebook) | LCC F1543.2 .K55 2020
    (print) | DDC 972.86–dc23
LC record available at https://lccn.loc.gov/2019001493

Editor: Rebecca Sabelko   Designer: Brittany McIntosh

Printed in the United States of America, North Mankato, MN.

TABLE OF CONTENTS

MONTEVERDE

A family arrives in Monteverde after driving up a narrow, winding road. It is a mild, humid morning in the **cloud forest**. Colorful butterflies flit about in the many trees. The family wanders through the mist of tumbling waterfalls.

OTHER TOP SITES

IRAZÚ VOLCANO

NICOYA PENINSULA

PRE-COLUMBIAN GOLD MUSEUM

TORTUGUERO NATIONAL PARK

Later, they join a wildlife tour at *Serpentario de Monteverde*. They see poison dart frogs and many different snakes. After a picnic lunch, they go zip-lining through the mountain **rain forest**. They fly past ferns, mosses, and vines. A **symphony** of bird calls fills the air. Welcome to Costa Rica!

Costa Rica is located in Central America. It covers 19,730 square miles (51,100 square kilometers). The nation's capital, San José, lies in the central valley along with other major cities, such as Alajuela and Cartago.

Nicaragua stretches along Costa Rica's northern border. All along the country's east coast are the turquoise waters of the Caribbean Sea. Panama is Costa Rica's neighbor to the southeast. The waves of the Pacific Ocean lap upon the shores of Costa Rica's entire western coast.

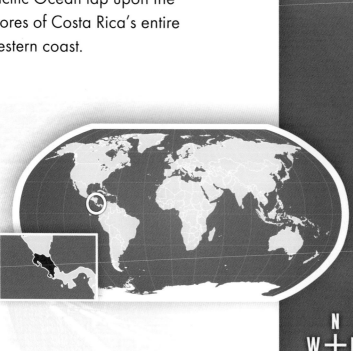

N
W E
S

NICARAGUA

CARIBBEAN
SEA

HEREDIA

ALAJUELA

LIMÓN

CARTAGO

SAN JOSÉ

COSTA RICA

PANAMA

PACIFIC
OCEAN

LANDSCAPE AND CLIMATE

Beautiful beaches dot the landscape along Costa Rica's Pacific coast. Northern Costa Rica is made up of **plains** and the rugged Nicoya **Peninsula**. The Cordillera Volcánica and Cordillera de Talamanca mountains run from north to south in the country's interior.

= CORDILLERA DE VOLCÁNICA
= CORDILLERA DE TALAMANCA
= MESETA CENTRAL

A highland area, the Meseta Central, lies between these mountain ranges. The Caribbean lowlands lie north and east of the central mountains.

CORDILLERA DE TALAMANCA

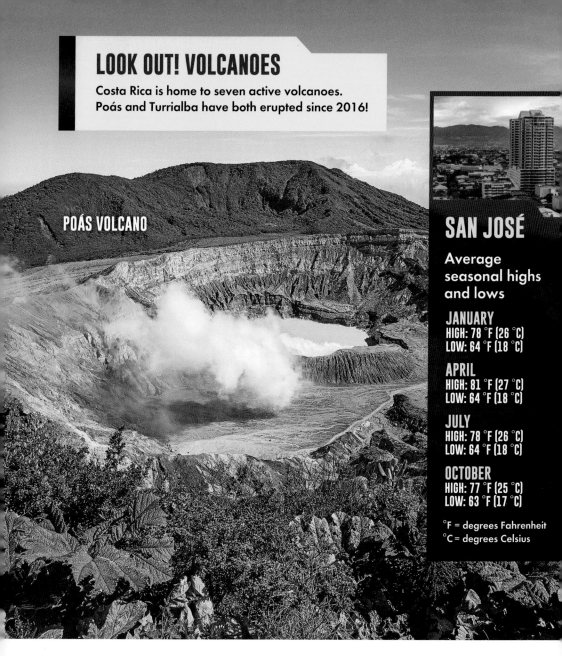

POÁS VOLCANO

SAN JOSÉ

Average seasonal highs and lows

JANUARY
HIGH: 78 °F (26 °C)
LOW: 64 °F (18 °C)

APRIL
HIGH: 81 °F (27 °C)
LOW: 64 °F (18 °C)

JULY
HIGH: 78 °F (26 °C)
LOW: 64 °F (18 °C)

OCTOBER
HIGH: 77 °F (25 °C)
LOW: 63 °F (17 °C)

°F = degrees Fahrenheit
°C = degrees Celsius

Costa Rica's climate has two seasons. The rainy season lasts from May to November while the dry season runs from December to April. Overall, the climate is **tropical** year-round. Temperatures tend to be cooler in the highland areas.

WILDLIFE

Costa Rica is home to a huge variety of wildlife. Humpback whales, dolphins, sea turtles, and manatees swim off the coasts. In the **volcanic** mountains of the north, brown-throated sloths and mantled howler monkeys move among the branches. Meanwhile, keel-billed toucans soar between trees. Near the border with Nicaragua, collared peccaries and pumas roam the forest. Crocodiles hunt in the waterways.

Strawberry poison frogs also live in Costa Rica's rain forests. Many reptiles do as well. Some, like coral snakes and bushmasters, are **venomous**.

BROWN-THROATED SLOTH

MANTLED HOWLER MONKEY

GREEN-CROWNED BRILLIANT HUMMINGBIRD

BEAUTIFUL BIRDS

Costa Rica is home to over 800 bird species. These include parrots, hummingbirds, and macaws. Many live in the nation's rain forests.

COLLARED PECCARY

STRAWBERRY
POISON FROG

STRAWBERRY
POISON FROG

Life Span: 3 to 15 years
Red List Status: least concern

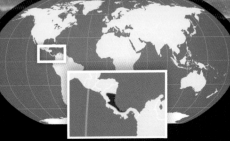

stawberry poison frog range =

LEAST CONCERN	NEAR THREATENED	VULNERABLE	ENDANGERED	CRITICALLY ENDANGERED	EXTINCT IN THE WILD	EXTINCT
▲						

Nearly 5 million Costa Ricans make homes in Costa Rica.
They often call themselves *ticos*. Most Costa Ricans have Spanish
ancestors. Many have **native** and European backgrounds.
They are also known as *mestizos*. Costa Rica's native groups
include the Bribri and Chorotega, among others. Some
Costa Ricans have Spanish, native, and African backgrounds.

Most Costa Ricans belong to the Roman Catholic Church. Others practice different forms of Christianity. About 1 out of 10 people do not follow any religion. Costa Rica's official language is Spanish.

FAMOUS FACE
Name: **Laura Chinchilla Miranda**
Birthday: **March 28, 1959**
Hometown: **Desamparados, Costa Rica**
Famous for: **The first woman president of Costa Rica, serving from 2010-2014**

SPEAK SPANISH

ENGLISH	SPANISH	HOW TO SAY IT
hello	hola	OH-lah
goodbye	adiós	ah-dee-OHS
please	por favor	pohr fah-VOR
thank you	gracias	grah-SEE-ahs
yes	sí	SEE
no	no	noh

SAN JOSÉ

COMMUNITIES

Most Costa Ricans live in **urban** areas, such as San José. People live in both apartment buildings and houses. City travel is often by bus. However, biking is becoming more popular. In the countryside, older homes may be built from **adobe**. But near the coastline, they are often made of wood. Some stand on stilts to prevent flooding. People in **rural** areas may travel by bus, train, or even boat.

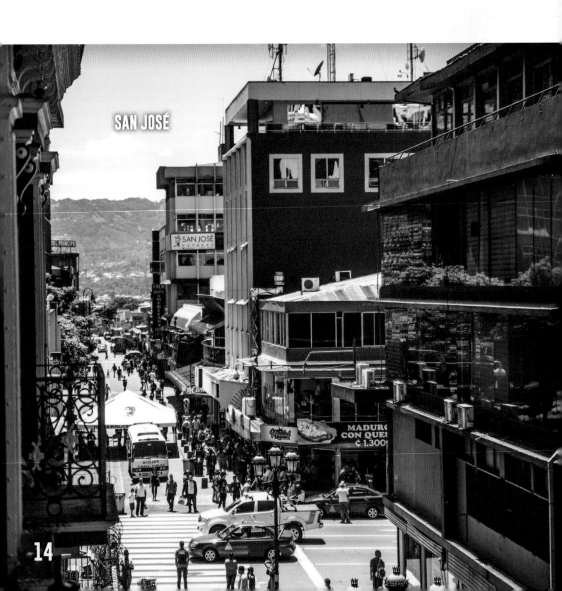

SAN JOSÉ

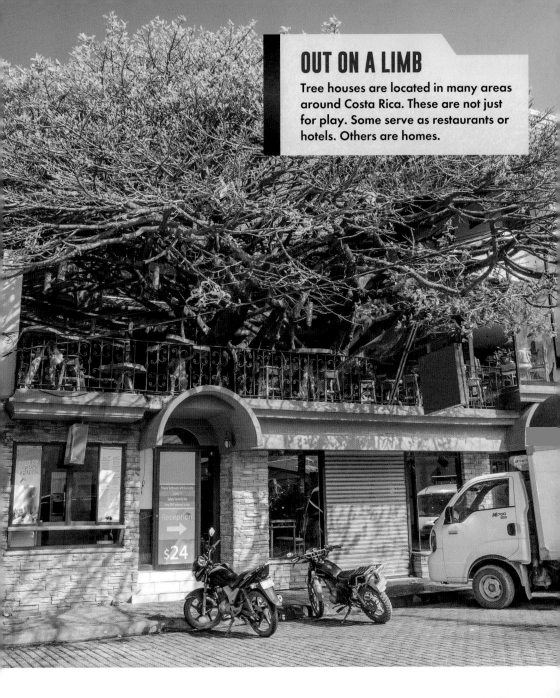

OUT ON A LIMB

Tree houses are located in many areas around Costa Rica. These are not just for play. Some serve as restaurants or hotels. Others are homes.

Family is very important in Costa Rica. It is common for children to live at home with their parents until they are married. Families are small, often with two children.

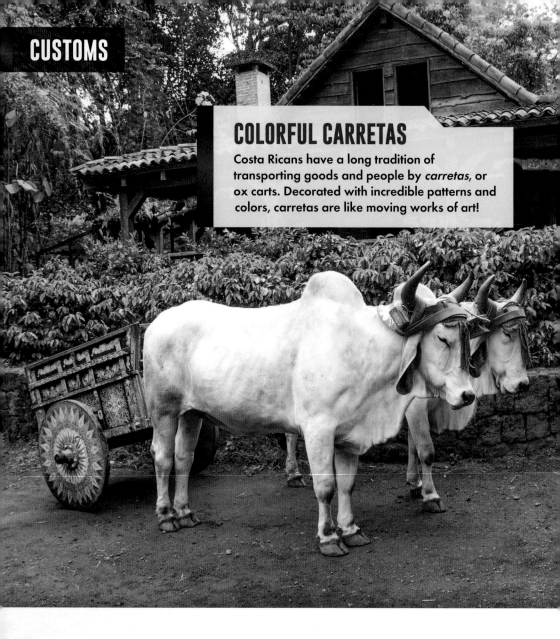

COLORFUL CARRETAS
Costa Ricans have a long tradition of transporting goods and people by *carretas*, or ox carts. Decorated with incredible patterns and colors, carretas are like moving works of art!

The phrase *pura vida*, or "pure life," is often used in Costa Rica. It describes the relaxed way of life. Ticos use the term to greet each other, say goodbye, or just let others know that life is good. Costa Ricans place a high value on education and **democracy**. They also tend to focus on the positive.

Throughout Costa Rica, people wear Western-style clothing. But shorts are only worn in beach areas or coastal cities. At rodeos, both women and men dress up like *vaqueros*, or cowboys. They wear jeans, hats, plaid shirts, and belts with big buckles.

VAQUERO

Students in Costa Rica begin school at age 6. Primary
education lasts through sixth grade, and most students go
on to attend secondary school. Some students choose to
further their education at universities or through **vocational**
programs. Costa Rica has over 50 universities for students
who have completed secondary school.

Nearly two out of three people have **service jobs**. They work in banks, hospitals, hotels, and national parks. Other Costa Ricans **manufacture** products like furniture, clothing, or medical equipment. Farmers grow bananas, coffee, pineapples, sugar, and other crops.

FARMER

LET'S PLAY BALL!
Every baseball used in Major League Baseball is made in Costa Rica. Each year the Rawlings factory in Turrialba produces almost 2.4 million baseballs!

SOCCER

Soccer is Costa Rica's most popular sport. Both kids and adults kick a ball around on nearly any empty field or patch of land. Huge crowds gather to watch professional teams play at San José's Saprissa Stadium. Ticos also enjoy basketball, tennis, and auto racing. Surfing and fishing are popular along the coasts. The country's many national parks draw hikers from around the globe.

HIKING

On weekends, people entertain themselves by going to shopping malls and movie theaters. Sundays are a popular day to visit family members and relax. City dwellers often travel to Costa Rica's mountains or beaches for vacations.

CHOROTEGA POTTERY

The Chorotega people from the Guanacaste province are famous for their pottery. It often features designs and pictures of animals.

What You Need:
- air-drying clay
- black, red, and/or white paint

Instructions:
1. Tear off a piece of the air-drying clay. Use your hands to shape it into a small jar or small plate.

2. Once you are happy with the shape of your object, set it aside to dry.

3. When the pottery is dry, paint some traditional designs or images on your object. Common shapes include spirals and triangles, and common animals include crocodiles, macaws, turtles, and monkeys.

4. Let the paint dry completely, then display your work someplace special!

Costa Ricans eat rice and beans at most meals. A typical breakfast is called *gallo pinto*, or "spotted rooster." It is made of rice, black beans, onions, and cilantro. People in Costa Rica eat a lot of soups and stews. *Olla de carne* is a beef stew that has onions, potatoes, and other vegetables.

Along the Caribbean coast, people cook with more spices. Cloves and chilies are popular. They also use coconut milk to flavor their dishes. People all over Costa Rica eat a variety of fruits. Bananas, pineapples, and mangoes are just a few favorites. Coffee is the most popular drink.

GALLO PINTO

OLLA DE CARNE

BLACK BEAN SOUP RECIPE

Black bean soup is a popular dish in Costa Rica. Try this easy recipe with the help of an adult!

Ingredients:

1/2 cup celery, finely diced
1 small onion, finely diced
1 small red or green bell pepper, finely diced
1 clove garlic, minced
1/2 tablespoon olive or canola oil
2 15-ounce cans black beans, including their liquid
1 1/2 cups vegetable broth
1/2 teaspoon oregano
1/2 teaspoon cumin
pinch of clove and nutmeg (optional)

Steps:

1. Put the celery, onion, pepper, garlic, and oil into a large saucepan. Cook over medium heat until all of the vegetables are soft and the onion is clear. This will take about 15-20 minutes.

2. Add the remaining ingredients to the pan. Bring everything to a boil, then turn the heat down so the soup simmers but does not boil.

Many of Costa Rica's celebrations are Christian holidays. Christmas is the biggest of them all! Costa Ricans often decorate fake evergreen trees and display them outside their homes for everyone to enjoy. Holy Week, known as *Semana Santa*, is the week before Easter. Some people take part in religious parades through their towns. Others travel to the beach or the mountains for vacation.

On September 15, Costa Ricans celebrate their nation's independence from Spain. Parades include decorated floats, marching bands, and giant masked puppets called *payasos*. All throughout the year, Costa Ricans celebrate their nation and **culture**!

CARNIVAL

In October, the city of Limón celebrates its Afro-Caribbean culture with Carnival. There is live music, dancing, and much more. At noon, fireworks remind people the party is starting.

INDEPENDENCE
DAY

1808
Coffee is introduced in Costa Rica and becomes an important crop

AROUND 1000 CE
Chorotega people arrive in what is today Costa Rica

1502
Christopher Columbus visits the area and names it Costa Rica

1821
Costa Rica gains independence from Spain

1564
The first permanent European settlement is built at Cartago

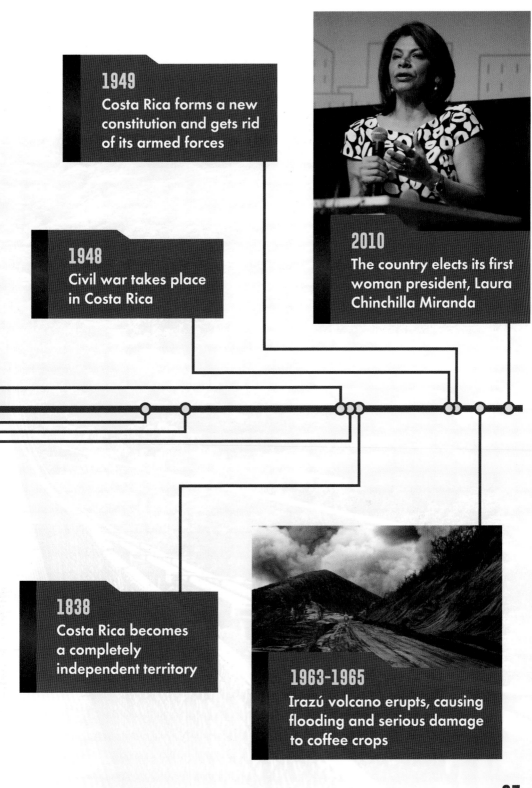

1949
Costa Rica forms a new constitution and gets rid of its armed forces

2010
The country elects its first woman president, Laura Chinchilla Miranda

1948
Civil war takes place in Costa Rica

1838
Costa Rica becomes a completely independent territory

1963-1965
Irazú volcano erupts, causing flooding and serious damage to coffee crops

COSTA RICA FACTS

Official Name: Republic of Costa Rica

Flag of Costa Rica: Costa Rica's flag has five horizontal bands of color. The top and bottom bands are blue, representing the sky, opportunity, and perseverance. The white bands symbolize peace, wisdom, and happiness. The central band is red, representing the blood that was shed for freedom. The coat of arms inside the red band includes three volcanoes, merchant ships, and a rising sun. The seven stars stand for the country's seven provinces.

Area: 19,730 square miles
(51,100 square kilometers)

Capital City: San José

Important Cities: Limón, Alajuela, Heredia

Population:
4,987,142 (July 2018 est.)

COUNTRYSIDE
20.7%

WHERE
PEOPLE LIVE

CITY
79.3%

JOBS

- SERVICES **64%**
- MANUFACTURING **22%**
- FARMING **14%**

Main Exports:

bananas

pineapples

coffee

medical equipment

National Holiday:
Independence Day (September 15)

Main Language:
Spanish

Form of Government:
presidential republic

Title for Country Leader:
president

RELIGION

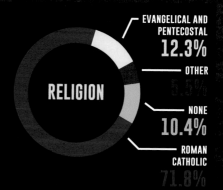

- EVANGELICAL AND PENTECOSTAL **12.3%**
- OTHER **5.5%**
- NONE **10.4%**
- ROMAN CATHOLIC **71.8%**

Unit of Money:
Costa Rican colón

GLOSSARY

adobe—bricks made of clay and straw that are dried in the sun

ancestors—relatives who lived long ago

cloud forest—a wet mountain forest located in a warm area, often with many clouds

culture—the beliefs, arts, and ways of life in a place or society

democracy—a system of government in which people choose the leaders

manufacture—to make products, often with machines

native—originally from the area or related to a group of people that began in the area

peninsula—a section of land that extends out from a larger piece of land and is almost completely surrounded by water

plains—large areas of flat land

rain forest—a thick, green forest that receives a lot of rain

rural—related to the countryside

service jobs—jobs that perform tasks for people or businesses

symphony—an arrangement of sounds

tropical—part of the tropics; the tropics is a hot, rainy region near the equator.

urban—related to cities and city life

venomous—producing a poisonous substance called venom

vocational—involved in the training of a skill or trade that prepares an individual for a career

volcanic—relating to a hole in the earth; when a volcano erupts, hot ash, gas, or melted rock called lava shoots out.

TO LEARN MORE

AT THE LIBRARY

Burns, Loree Griffin. *Handle with Care: An Unusual Butterfly Journey.* Minneapolis, Minn.: Millbrook Press, 2014.

Kopp, Megan. *Costa Rica.* New York, N.Y.: AV2 by Weigl, 2018.

Vargas, Maxine. *The People and Culture of Costa Rica.* New York, N.Y.: PowerKids Press, 2018.

ON THE WEB

FACTSURFER

Factsurfer.com gives you a safe, fun way to find more information.

1. Go to www.factsurfer.com.

2. Enter "Costa Rica" into the search box and click 🔍.

3. Select your book cover to see a list of related web sites.

INDEX

The images in this book are reproduced through the courtesy of: Simon Dannhauer, cover; Andrzej Rostek, pp. 4-5; alexilena, p. 5 (top); Hugo Brizard - YouGoPhoto, p. 5 (top middle); Jorge Tutor/ Alamy, p. 5 (bottom middle); SL-Photography, p. 5 (bottom); AridOcean, pp. 6-7, 8; DeAgostini/ Alamy, p. 8 (back); Michal Sarauer, p. 9; mbrand85, p. 9 (right); Sean R. Stubben, p. 10 (left); Fireglow, p. 10 (top); Elliotte Rusty Harold, p. 10 (middle); Ondrej Prosicky, p. 10 (bottom); dirk Ercken, pp. 10-11; Sergi Reboredo/ Alamy, p. 12; Sueddeutsche Zeitung Photo/ Alamy, p. 13 (top); ShutterStockStudio, p. 13; Luis Alvarado Alvarado, p. 14; Mario Gyß/ Alamy, p. 15; spacaj, p. 16; Michael Dwyer/ Alamy, p. 17; Alex Robinson/ Getty, p. 18; JHVEPhoto, p. 19 (top); Juan Carlos Ulate/ Newscom, p. 19; Laszlo Szirtesi/ Alamy, p. 20 (top); Rob Crandall/ Alamy, p. 20; iFerol, p. 21 (top); Driendl Group/ Getty, p. 21; Mostardi Photography/ Alamy, p. 22; AS Food Studio, p. 23 (top); Marco Diaz Degura, p. 23 (middle); StockphotoVideo, p. 23 (bottom); Ezequiel Becerra/ Getty, p. 24; Cara Koch, p. 25; GCapture, p. 26; EFE New Agency/ Alamy, p. 27 (top); InterFoto/ Alamy, p. 27; Ivsanmas, p. 28; imageBroker/ Alamy, p. 29; Andrey Lobachev, p. 29 (right).